Croome Park

WORCESTERSHIRE

A souvenir guide

National Trust

THE FIRST LANDSCAPE GARDEN

WHERE IT ALL BEGAN

The 18th-century landscape garden has been called Britain's greatest contribution to the visual arts. Croome was the first garden designed from the start in this 'natural' style. Every element was carefully considered and integrated: house and church, garden buildings and statues, river and lake, parkland and pleasure grounds, trees and shrubs, all set against the stunning backdrop of the Malverns. A network of meandering paths and longer carriage drives led from one viewing point to the next, where the eye was drawn to 'eye-catchers' near and far. Croome was to prove immensely influential, transforming the landscape of Britain.

'And, here, gradually opening before the surprised and delighted view – stretching in a wide circumference – appears a scene of rural beauty and grandeur, rarely surpassed; in which, wood, water, and ornamental buildings, aided by pleasing inequalities of ground, combine to produce a finely picturesque and powerful effect.'

1824 Croome guidebook

Left *Croome Park*; by Richard Wilson, 1758 (Croome Estate Trustees). Wilson's painting shows the south front of the house from across the river, which is spanned by William Halfpenny's Chinese Bridge of 1750–1 (demolished after 1905; to be restored by the National Trust). It also includes, on the ridge to the right, the Rotunda and to the left, the church, although the latter had not yet been built in 1758

Out of a morass

The place took its name from the stream that flowed sluggishly through a shallow, low-lying valley with a ridge to the east and the Malvern Hills to the west (in Old English, *Crombe* means 'a winding stream'). The soil is heavy clay marl, and the ground boggy. It seems an unpromising spot for a garden.

Think again.

The makers of Croome

Croome was the brain child of **George William, 6th Earl of Coventry**, whose wealth and ambition matched his good taste. Having swept away the earlier formal garden, he remade the landscape of his ancestral estate between 1747 and his death in 1809. The 6th Earl brought together at Croome three of the finest designers of the late 18th century: 'Capability' Brown, Robert Adam and James Wyatt. When *'Capability' Brown* arrived at Croome in 1752, he was just starting out on his independent career as a landscape gardener. What he achieved here provided the template for all his later work on the great estates of Britain. *Robert Adam* applied his delicate brand of Neo-classicism to Croome's garden buildings and to the interior of the house. He also provided Gothic designs for decorating the new church. *James Wyatt* carried on where Adam had left off, enriching the Pleasure Grounds and wider landscape with further elegant buildings, bridges and gates mostly in a Neo-classical style.

Water garden, world garden

Brown's landscape was designed to look natural, but it depended as much on engineering as on art or nature. To drain the 'morass', miles of culverts had to be dug, and a new river and lake created. And to beautify the newly fertile landscape, Brown depended not just on native trees and shrubs, but on hundreds of exotic species recently introduced to Britain by plant-hunters from across the world. By the 1820s, Croome was second only to Kew in its botanical diversity.

Restoring Croome

The 6th Earl's descendants were happy to enjoy what he had created without radically altering it. The house and Pleasure Grounds were sold in 1948, and by the time the National Trust acquired 324 hectares (800 acres) of the parkland in 1996 with the generous help of the Heritage Lottery Fund and Royal & SunAlliance, the Pleasure Grounds were suffering from many years of intensive agriculture and the intrusion of the M5. However, the key elements were still intact, and the rich estate archive (now in the Worcestershire Record Office) also survived. After careful research, the National Trust has been methodically piecing the mosaic back together again.

Above The 6th Earl of Coventry; by Allan Ramsay

Below The Temple Greenhouse in 1903

TOUR OF THE PLEASURE GROUNDS

VISITOR RECEPTION
The National Trust's reception buildings have been converted from the World War II Station Sick Quarters attached to RAF Defford.

THE WILDERNESS WALK
This curving path was densely planted with trees and shrubs, including roses and honeysuckle, to create a scented walk from the arboretum to the church. It was replanted by the National Trust in 1999 following an 1824 plan by the leading garden designer J.C. Loudon. The walk was well-known for its truffles.

GEORGIAN GOTHIC: THE CHURCH OF ST MARY MAGDALENE
The 6th Earl considered the medieval church too close to the house, and so demolished it. He decided to rebuild on high ground 500 metres to the north-east. 'Capability' Brown produced a classical design in 1758, but, probably on the advice of his friend Sanderson Miller, the 6th Earl opted for Gothic. Brown was almost certainly responsible for designing the exterior, which is dominated by the west tower. The tower served as both a viewing platform and as an 'eye-catcher' in many of the

'The Stranger is next conducted into the Wilderness Walk – winding among the natural columns of closely-planted trees; twisting their branches together, in many a rude fantastic form; and extending a rich canopy of foliage, over the head. It is a pleasant retreat – at all times, agreeable – but, in the glare of noon-day, in the heat of summer, it must be peculiarly refreshing and delightful.'

1824 guidebook

Right The church was carefully placed to catch the eye

views from the Pleasure Grounds. The interior was designed by Robert Adam in a delicate Georgian Gothic style. He used trusted craftsmen to carry out the work: Joseph Rose for the ceiling plasterwork; Sefferin Alken and John Hobcroft for the intricate pulpit. Adam proposed stained glass for the east window, but this seems not to have been carried out. The church was consecrated on 29 June 1763 to St Mary Magdalene, perhaps in memory of the 6th Earl's first wife, Maria, who was reburied here. The pews have been rearranged and altered, but otherwise the church has changed little since the 6th Earl's time. It is now in the care of the Churches Conservation Trust.

Below The church in 1784; watercolour by E.F. and T.F. Burney
Below right The interior of the church

Monuments
The 6th Earl moved the substantial tombs of four of his 17th-century ancestors from the old church to the chancel. The Earl himself is remembered by a tablet on the south wall.

THE CHURCH SHRUBBERY
Among those buried in the nearby graveyard is William Dean, who was head gardener from 1801 to 1831 and contributed to the 1824 guidebook to Croome.

THE ICE-HOUSE
South of the church are the ruins of the domed brick ice-house. Insulated by its thatched roof, it would have provided ice to the house through the summer. It was still in use in 1915 and has recently been restored.

THE HOUSE

Croome Court lies surprisingly low in the landscape for an 18th-century country house. The obvious position was where the church now is, but the 6th Earl decided to rebuild on the foundations of the previous, early 1640s house, retaining the core of the old building, together with the somewhat overbearing chimneystacks.

His architect was 'Capability' Brown, who had hitherto built very little, and the marked similarities to Hagley Hall, which was designed by Sanderson Miller, suggest that the 6th Earl's friend may also been involved. The new house was built in 1752–62 from warm Bath stone in a rather ponderous Palladian style, with four large corner turrets. The house's relation to the landscape is more subtle: the Long Gallery, which occupies the entire west front, enjoys superb views over the river and the Pleasure Grounds. The house itself also features in many of the key vistas.

Opposite, top A bird's-eye view of the 17th-century house and the old church (now gone) in 1750

Below The north front of the house from the church in 1784; watercolour by E.F. and T.F. Burney

'Leaving the Church – the Stranger will naturally pause – to contemplate, from its high grounds, the grand prospect, which again bursts, in full display, before him – offering a grand near view of the House, seated in the vale below – thence extending over the lawns, the woods, and the waters, of the park – shut in by the long waving line of the Malvern hills, melting into the wide horizon.'

1824 guidebook

Right South front of the house from the river in 1824. On the left are the church and William Halfpenny's Chinese bridge (now gone)

THE EVERGREEN SHRUBBERY

A curving path leads down from the church to the lake. On either side, Brown created dense shrubberies on the site of the demolished medieval village, choosing evergreen species from all over the world. Brown's scheme was replanted in 2003, but it will be several years before the enclosed effect he intended has been re-created.

The *statue of Pan* was put up about 1800. It was discovered in the undergrowth in the 1970s and has recently been returned after restoration. According to the 1824 guidebook, 'That great patron of rural pursuits and rural pleasures … would have no cause to be dissatisfied with the situation in which a figure of himself is placed.' In 1824 four statues of the Seasons also stood here, but these no longer survive.

THE TEMPLE GREENHOUSE

Built from Painswick limestone in 1760, this was Robert Adam's first garden building at Croome. Adam charged £15 and also supplied designs for garden stools with lion's-paw feet in 1765. The Temple Greenhouse was used to display tender exotics from the 6th Earl's extensive collection. In winter, they were protected by large sash-windows, made by Hobcroft (now gone, but look out for the slots in the floor), and by underfloor heating fed by a furnace in the brick bothy which was added to the back of the building about 1762. The sash-windows were stored in the bothy during the summer.

The *pediment* is decorated with a basket and festoons of fruit and flowers, which were richly carved in 1765 by Sefferin Alken, who also made the plaques of horns of plenty over the windows. The windows were originally niches for lead sculptures by John Cheere of Ceres and Flora – appropriately, goddesses of the harvest and flowers – which were supplied in 1763.

To the south-west of the Temple Greenhouse are the foundations of the *privy*, which was provided in 1765 for visitors who were caught short in the garden.

Left The Temple Greenhouse in 1784; watercolour by E.F. and T.F. Burney

'Delightfully sheltered, beneath the umbrageous arms of spreading trees, appears an elegant modern TEMPLE, open in front, supported by plain Doric pillars; from each side of which, the pleasure grounds are seen, extending in a long range.'

1824 guidebook

'This ... shrubbery is formed by a vast variety of evergreens, assembled and massed together; affording a cool sequestered retreat, in summer; but which would be peculiarly grateful, as a winter walk.'

1824 guidebook

Left The Temple Greenhouse in 1824, showing the sash-windows and shrubs in pots; from the Croome guidebook

Below The Temple Greenhouse today

THE DRUID

The Coade-stone statue of the Druid was supplied in 1795 for 24 guineas. It stands on a Neo-classical pedestal designed by Wyatt in 1796. Many 18th-century gardens included reminders of Britain's prehistoric past in the form of grottoes, hermitages and other simple structures thought to have been inhabited by Druids. Druids also had a political significance, symbolising ancient British liberty.

THE DRY ARCH BRIDGE

This tunnel was built so that visitors to the Pleasure Grounds could reach the lake without having to cross the busy carriage drive from Worcester to the house, which ran across the top. The vermiculated (resembling worm-casts) façades of the bridge and the keystones, which feature the heads of river gods (one dated 1797), are made of Coade stone. The bridge was designed by Brown, probably in the 1760s, and remodelled by Wyatt in the late 1790s.

Right Coade-stone keystone of a river god on the Dry Arch Bridge

Below The Dry Arch Bridge

THE HA-HA

Many 18th-century landscape gardens included a sunk fence of this kind in order to provide uninterrupted views from the house over the surrounding countryside. The Croome ha-ha, which was dug in 1765, is unusual in that it faces both inwards and outwards – an acknowledgement that the views from the Pleasure Grounds towards the house were just as important as those looking outwards.

THE FERRY CROSSING

Near the Dry Arch Bridge is an iron bridge, which was put up in the 1970s. Originally, visitors crossed the river in a ferry pulled by rope. You can still see the steps of the landing point here.

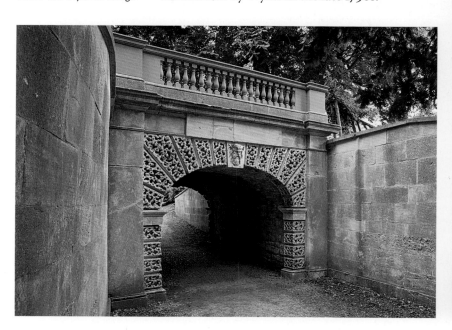

Mrs Coade's stone

Eleanor Coade (1733–1821) marketed a type of stoneware which could be cast into statues, urns and other garden ornaments. When double-fired, it resembled Portland stone and was durable enough to survive the worst of the British climate. She sold a huge range of designs from her factory in Lambeth and was the most successful businesswoman of the late 18th century.

Below Etching of the Druid, from Mrs Coade's 1778 catalogue **Right** The Druid

'The figure of a DRUID soon appears; resting on a pedestal; and placed under the shade of a large oak; a tree, which, it is well known, the priests of that ancient order held in high veneration; and which they selected, above all others, in the formation of their sacred groves.... Clusters of shrubs of every kind, and borders of flowers of every hue and scent, conspire with the fine over-hanging shade to communicate all the delight, which beautiful sylvan scenes can afford.'

1824 guidebook

THE RIVER

The river is the key to the Croome landscape. Work started on creating it before 'Capability' Brown arrived, and the first phase, which was supervised by John Phipps, was completed in 1748. In 1750 Lord Bateman wrote admiringly to the future 6th Earl: 'You have made a River where no water ever *ran* before.' Brown extended the river and made it flow in a serpentine arc to the west of the house, mirroring the course of the Severn a mile to the west. He also gave the river banks a gently sloping profile so that the 6th Earl's pedigree cattle could drink from the water's edge. However, a horse-driven pump was needed to maintain the water level in summer. As late as 1780 Brown was still tinkering with the watercourses, and in 1796 the 6th Earl called in the Birmingham canal engineer John Snape to make further adjustments.

THE LAKE

At the west end of the river is the lake, in a formerly boggy spot known as Seggy Mere. Brown dug out the bog and extended the river to connect with it. The lake became the focus of the Pleasure Grounds, with a series of paths leading from one carefully contrived viewing point to the next, where visitors would halt to enjoy the spectacle of trees, shrubs and monuments reflected in the still, but clear waters of the lake.

Below The serpentine river

Right The lake

THE ISLAND PAVILION

This chaste little garden shelter and picnic spot was built in 1776–8, possibly to a design by Adam. The Corinthian capitals are Coade stone, as are the low-relief plaques, which were installed in 1778 and depict the Aldobrandini wedding (in the centre), griffins and Phrygian shepherds. The building had suffered grievous vandalism and required careful restoration by the National Trust.

THE BRIDGES

The first of the wrought-iron bridges was built by John Mackell in 1795 replacing wooden ones linking the islands with the rest of the Pleasure Grounds. They have recently been restored.

THE BOATHOUSE

At the south end of the lake are the brick foundations of one of Croome's two boathouses. It was designed by Brown and had a low thatched roof. Rowing boats and a pleasure barge, painted in the Coventry colours of blue and vermilion, were moored in the dock. Boating was a popular amusement for the 6th Earl and his guests.

Left A view across the island to the house

Below The Island Pavilion

13

THE GROTTO

This is one of Brown's later contributions to the garden: work began here in 1765. The Grotto forms a curving screen constructed of roughly cut blocks of limestone, tufa and Daglingworth stone. Between 1781 and 1786 it was covered with tropical shells, corals, semi-precious stones, 'Derbyshire Petrifications', fossils and polished pebbles, which would have sparkled in the sunlight. Today, we associate grottoes with Santa Claus, but traditionally they were considered to be the home of water-nymphs. Hence the Latin inscription from Virgil's epic poem, *The Aeneid*, which is also found in the grotto at Stourhead. It translates: 'Behold! A cave beneath the overhanging rocks. Inside, fresh-water springs, and seats formed from the living stone. This is the home of the Nymphs!'

SABRINA

Below The Grotto

The reclining Coade-stone figure represents Sabrina, who, according to the medieval chronicler Geoffrey of Monmouth, was a water-nymph inhabiting the River Severn (Sabrina is Latin for Severn). Sabrina is part of the foundation myth of Britain, which told how the ancient Britons were descended from the classical hero Brutus, great-grandson of Aeneas of Troy. She also appears in Milton's masque *Comus*:

> Sabrina fair,
> Listen where thou art sitting
> Under the glassy, cool translucent wave.

The statue, which cost 30 guineas, was added in 1804. It was probably designed by John Bacon, who also produced the 6th Earl's monument in Croome church. It has recently been conserved, but the waterworks have still to be put back.

At night, the effect would have been even more magical, as Sabrina would have been lit by a lamp hanging from an iron hook (still visible above).

'Beyond the Grotto, appears the figure of a Water Nymph, reclining on the bank, and holding an urn – through which, the waters, collected from a copious spring, at some distance, are made to flow.'

1824 guidebook

Opposite Sabrina

Above The Monument to 'Capability' Brown. The inscription reads: *'To the memory of Lancelot Brown who, by the powers of his inimitable and creative genius, formed this garden scene out of a morass.'*

THE WORCESTER GATES

The gates mark the point at which you enter the Pleasure Grounds on the carriage drive from Worcester. They were designed by Adam and modified by Wyatt in 1793–4. They are topped by shallow urns and decorated with Coade-stone festoons. Both sides of the drive would have been densely planted, delaying the moment of maximum drama, when you first catch sight of the house, until you cross the Dry Arch Bridge (see p.10).

THE MONUMENT TO 'CAPABILITY' BROWN

The casket on a Coade-stone pedestal commemorates Brown's achievement at Croome and his friendship with the 6th Earl, who erected it in 1797. It was demolished by a falling tree in 1972, but restored by the National Trust.

Nearby is a more modest memorial to Brown's biographer, Dorothy Stroud (1910–97).

Above left The Worcester Lodge Gates in 1784; watercolour by E.T. and T.F. Burney

Opposite The Worcester Lodge Gates today

THE WIDER LANDSCAPE

THE PARK SEAT

Standing at the southern end of the Croome river one mile from the Pleasure Grounds, the Park Seat was intended as an elegant little shelter and viewing point, from which you could enjoy the other principal eye-catchers on the estate. It was also known as the Owl's Nest, after a temporary occupant. Adam provided an initial design in 1766, but the 6th Earl wanted something simpler, and it was not finally built until 1770–2. It has recently been restored by the National Trust, complete with a new iron gate.

Left The Park Seat

THE ROTUNDA

The Rotunda stands in the Home Shrubbery on the lias ridge to the east of the house. It was built in 1754–7 to a design by Brown, who also planted the older cedars that still shelter it. John Hobcroft was responsible for the joinery, and Francesco Vasalli for the stuccowork. Six Portland stone panels carved by Sefferin Alken to Adam's design, were added in 1763. The views from here of Bredon and the Malvern Hills are particularly fine.

OPPOSITE
Top The Rotunda
Bottom The Rotunda in 1824

'Seated on its proud eminence, the ROTUNDA presents itself to view.... It is an elegant stone building; plain in its exterior, but richly ornamented within: furnished with sofas, and fitted-up, as a summer evening apartment. A pleasing assemblage of trees, among which are the cypress and the cedar of Lebanon form with their blended foliage a woody crescent, encircling and sheltering it. But its great charm is its fine prospect.'

1824 guidebook

PIRTON CASTLE

Pirton Castle was designed by Wyatt and built by William Stephens in 1797 as an ivy-clad Gothic ruin. Thomas Whateley explained its purpose in his *Observations on Modern Gardening* (1770): 'Whatever building we see in decay, we naturally contrast its present to its former state and delight to ruminate on the comparison. It is true that such effects properly belong to real ruins; but they are produced in a certain degree by those which are fictitious; the impressions are not so strong, but they are exactly similar.'

'The ruins of Pirton Castle ... occupy a fine situation, on a lofty eminence; commanding from its high grounds, beautiful and extensive prospects.'

1824 guidebook

Below Wyatt's 1801 design for Pirton Castle

THE PANORAMA TOWER

The Panorama Tower was intended to be not only a viewing platform from which to follow the hunt, but also one of the principal eye-catchers in the views from the Pleasure Grounds. In addition, it offered views back to the house and church and over the Malverns. It was designed by Wyatt in 1801 following an Adam design, but was not built until 1805–12.

DUNSTALL CASTLE

Dunstall Castle was designed by Adam in 1765 as a mock-medieval ruin. It stands on Dunstall Common a mile south of the house, from which it was originally visible. In 1765 Adam wrote to the 6th Earl, 'I think it might be built to have a good effect at a Distance at no great Expense, as there does not require much delicacy in the workmanship.' L-shaped in plan, it combines round-headed and pointed windows. It was built in 1765–8 by the mason Robert Newman, who altered the central tower in 1771.

Far left, top Wyatt's 1801 design for the Panorama Tower, and **Below** The Panorama Tower today

Left Dunstall Castle in 1784; watercolour by E.T. and T.F. Burney, and **Below** Dunstall Castle today

CREATING CROOME

'A GRAVE YOUNG LORD'
GEORGE WILLIAM, 6TH EARL OF COVENTRY (1722–1809)

'Sacred to him the Genius of this place

Who reared these shades and formed these sweet retreats

With every incense breathing shrub adorned

And flower of faintest hue

His cultured tastes and native fancy bathed the scene around.'

From the monument to the 6th Earl

Above The 6th Earl of Coventry; by Allan Ramsay (Croome Estate Trust)

Right Maria, Countess of Coventry; by J.-E. Liotard (Musée d'Art et d'Histoire, Geneva). She was famous for her beauty and lack of tact. When the King asked her what she would most like to see in London, she replied, 'A coronation'

The 6th Earl was a younger son and so had never expected to inherit Croome. But in 1744 his elder brother died unexpectedly, making George William the heir to the estate. Their father, the 5th Earl, lived on until 1751, but he seems to have lost interest in Croome after this tragedy, and left George William to run the place.

The 6th Earl was a serious-minded and proud man – proud in particular of his taste. In the 18th century, good taste implied knowledge and patronage of the arts, but without vulgar extravagance. He was always careful with money, often querying tradesmen's bills, but he was also ambitious to beautify Croome, and his head gardener, William Dean, calculated that he spent the colossal sum of £400,000 to achieve this. He never made the Grand Tour of Europe, and seems to have learnt most from two cultured friends, Sanderson Miller of Radway and Richard Bateman of Shobdon, both of whom were amateur architects with a pioneering interest in reviving the Gothic style. Transforming Croome served the 6th Earl's political ambitions. He was elected MP for Worcestershire and was much involved in the affairs of the county, working to improve local turnpike roads and canals at the same time as he was remodelling the landscape and waterways of Croome. For much of the 1750s he was away in London at the court of George II, where he was swept up in the fashionable life of the capital. In 1751 his eye was caught by the beautiful young Maria Gunning, who, with her sister Elizabeth, caused the celebrity sensation of that season. After a whirlwind romance, they were married in March 1752. The first cracks started appearing during their honeymoon in Paris, where he is said to have chased her round the dining-table with a napkin, trying to wipe off the rouge he suspected her of wearing. But they patched things up, and he was grief-stricken when she died in 1760 aged only 28, her beauty ravaged by the effects of TB. He committed his feelings to verse:

Her noble Partner 'midst his Mansion Mourns
Now treads at Evg the dusky Vale forlorn.

In 1764 the 6th Earl married Barbara St John, who was an altogether easier person than Maria and much more interested in Croome. The new

Countess took an active part in tracking down rare plants for the garden and had her own model farm, dairy and menagerie – the last stocked with 'Sparrows of Paradise, Red headed Parrakeets, a Snow Bird and Silver Pheasants'.

The fame of Croome spread rapidly across the country, attracting the curious from near and far. The Pleasure Grounds became the setting for al fresco banquets, boating parties and firework displays. The seal was set on Croome's reputation in 1788, when George III and a large royal party toured the grounds. The 6th Earl lived long enough to see his planting reach maturity and was justifiably proud of what he had created, although he came to resent the loss of privacy that Croome's fame threatened.

Below, left Barbara, Countess of Coventry, the 6th Earl's second wife; by Allan Ramsay (Croome Estate Trust)

Below A nurseryman's plant bill to the 6th Earl, 20 March 1770

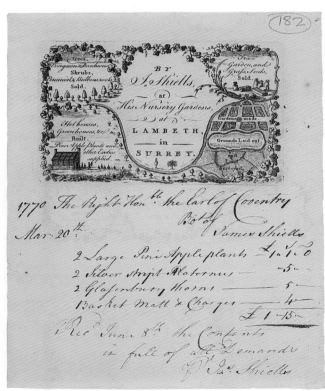

'MY FIRST AND FAVOURITE CHILD': 'CAPABILITY' BROWN (1716–83)

Lancelot Brown was 35 when he arrived at Croome in 1752, having been recommended to the 6th Earl by Sanderson Miller. He had spent the previous ten years working as head gardener at Stowe in Buckinghamshire, the most famous garden of the previous generation. Having developed a new, more apparently natural style of landscape in Stowe's Grecian Valley, he was ready to strike out on his own. But Brown was employed first at Croome, not as a gardener, but as an architect, designing the new house. He subsequently built the Rotunda, the exterior of the new church and the Grotto.

Smooth and serpentine

Brown turned his attention to the landscape about six years after the 6th Earl inherited the title and the estate in 1751. Croome engaged all Brown's talents as a landscape gardener, not only for earth-moving and tree-planting, but also for working with water. He extended the drainage scheme the Earl already had in hand, building brick culverts to channel water away from the house into a new river and lake. The river was redirected into a gently meandering course which now looks perfectly natural, but which in fact followed the serpentine 'line of beauty' that 18th-century taste recommended. The mirror-like surfaces of the river and lake reflected the smooth profile of the parkland and the contrasting shapes of the artfully placed garden buildings and trees.

Brown's work at Croome, which was in two main phases (1752–6, 1762–6), made his reputation and was never bettered in all his numerous later commissions.

Above 'Capability' Brown; by Nathaniel Dance, c.1769 (National Portrait Gallery)

Right Sanderson Miller (1716-80) was a gentleman architect who had been a friend of the 6th Earl since their student days. As well as recommending 'Capability' Brown, he advised the Earl on his Gothic buildings and drainage schemes, having perfected both on his Radway estate in Warwickshire. In 1747 the Earl wrote to Miller of 'various Projects in my head to embellish this untoward place which I wou'd not execute without your Taste.'

Inimitable genius

The 6th Earl got on well with Brown, writing in 1752, 'Mr Brown has done very well by me, and indeed I think has studied both my Place and my Pocket, which are not always conjunctively the Objects of Prospectors.' Their business relationship gradually warmed into friendship, and over the following 30 years Brown returned again and again to his 'first and favourite child', as he called it. When he collapsed and died in 1783, he was on the way home from supper at the 6th Earl's London home. The Earl paid tribute to Brown's 'inimitable genius' on the monument he put up in the garden in 1797.

Left 'Capability' Brown constructed a huge network of culverts to drain the marshy landscape

Below The Grecian Valley at Stowe

25

ROBERT ADAM (1728–92)

Adam first came to Croome in 1760, two years after he had returned from Italy, where his study of the surviving monuments of antiquity had furnished him with a new classical architectural language that was to dominate British taste for the next two decades. But the 6th Earl's first commission was to provide, not classical, but Gothic designs for the interior of Brown's new church. Adam created a delicate masterpiece of Georgian Gothic, embracing ceiling plasterwork, pulpit, font, pews and stained glass (only the last was not executed).

Left Robert Adam

The 6th Earl was so pleased with the result that he gave Adam a much bigger job – finishing off and refurnishing the inside of the house in the latest style, even though it was less than ten years old. Adam designed everything: plasterwork, panelling, fireplaces, mirrors, tables, chairs, sofas, commodes, a domed bed for the second Countess, and grand mahogany bookcases for the Earl's distinguished library (now in the Victoria & Albert Museum). The climax of the state rooms was the lavish Tapestry Room (now in the Metropolitan Museum in New York) and the Long Gallery

Below, left Robert Adam's London Arch; watercolour by E.T. and T.F. Burney

Below An Adam fireplace in Croome Court

with niches for classical statues. Adam went on to transform the 6th Earl's London house, no.106 Piccadilly, in the same way. The exteriors of both houses were left untouched – setting the pattern for Adam's later career, when he was usually asked to work within existing structures.

Adam had more freedom to exercise his architectural talents in the garden, designing the Temple Greenhouse, Island Pavilion, the Park Seat and the London Arch in his Neo-classical style. Occasionally, his proposals (for example, for the Countess's menagerie) were rejected as too elaborate and expensive. But although there were arguments about bills, architect and client remained on good terms over more than 30 years, and when Adam died in 1792, the 6th Earl served as one of the pall-bearers at his funeral.

JAMES WYATT (1746–1813)

The 6th Earl was in his seventies when Adam died, and might have been expected to call a halt to beautifying Croome. But he still wanted to do more and turned to James Wyatt as the most successful architect of the post-Adam generation to achieve it. Wyatt was employed at Croome between about 1793 and 1805. He worked mostly in a refined Neo-classical style, remodelling some of Brown and Adam's garden buildings and also introducing major new features such as the Panorama Tower and the sham Gothic ruin known as Pirton Castle. He was particularly keen on Coade stone, ordering statues and architectural decoration for the garden in this attractive and practical material (see p.11).

Below Map of Croome Park drawn up in 1796 by the canal engineer John Snape, who did further drainage work for the 6th Earl

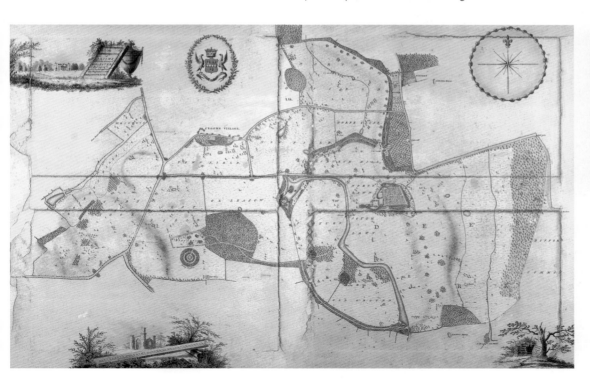

Above James Wyatt

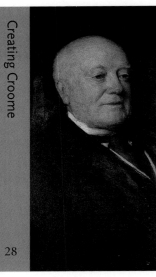

THE BLIND EARL

The 6th Earl fell out badly with his eldest son and heir, also named George William (1758–1831), who was not welcome at Croome. After the 7th Earl inherited the estate in 1809, he completed the construction of Wyatt's Panorama Tower and cherished the Pleasure Grounds, despite being unable to enjoy their visual delights, having been blinded in a hunting accident in 1780. The 1824 guidebook, with its eulogistic tour of the house and Pleasure Grounds and William Dean's

28

Left The 9th Earl of Coventry; by Percy Bigland
Below The Pleasure Grounds in 1903

extensive plant list (the *Hortus Croomensis*), confirms that the garden was still being kept up in all its magnificence. The 7th Earl took advice from the great landscape gardener Humphry Repton on the landscaping of his villa in Streatham, but seems not to have employed him at Croome.

However, the slow economic decline of Croome had already begun. Matters worsened during the brief, unhappy reign of the 8th Earl (1784–1843), whose miserable personal life and disastrous political career precipitated a complete mental collapse at the end of his life.

THE 9TH EARL

The 9th Earl (1838–1930) inherited Croome in 1843 at the age of only five, and was to live here for the next 88 years. The years of his minority allowed the estate a breathing space, in which it was able to recover partially from two decades of neglect. An 1844 survey of the estate (which comprised 16,000 acres in Worcestershire alone) led to a long-overdue programme of repairs to the house and garden buildings. The 9th Earl's coming of age in 1859 was celebrated on the estate with fireworks and a ton of plum pudding. Responding to the loyal toasts, he declared that 'he was ardently attached to the country, and he should be pleased to spend his days in the midst of an affectionate tenantry, and in the domain of his ancestors'. The house became a much-loved, cluttered home at the heart of a large rural community, and the 9th Earl conscientiously performed his duties as a paternalistic landlord, racehorse owner and huntsman. The kitchen and flower gardens continued to thrive, particularly after John Hill became the 9th Earl's agent in 1868. But Croome could not escape the depression that overwhelmed British agriculture from the 1870s. The 9th Earl attempted to carry on in the old ways, but towards the end of his long life he realised that things would have to change. In 1921 he set up the Croome Estate Trust to preserve it as a whole as an asset for his descendants. The trustees continued to run the estate for the next two decades, until war intervened.

CROOME AT WAR

The Second World War left its mark on Croome and the Coventrys. In May 1940 the 10th Earl was killed in action while serving with the Worcestershire Regiment during the retreat to Dunkirk. The following year, the eastern part of Croome Park was requisitioned by the RAF to form a new airfield. RAF Defford was used by Wellington bombers until 1942, when the Telecommunications Flying Unit arrived to conduct flight trials of top-secret radar technology. At the height of the war, over 2,500 servicemen and women were stationed here. The buildings now converted into the National Trust's visitor reception served as the base's hospital. Croome Court itself was occupied by Queen Juliana and the rest of the exiled Dutch royal family.

THE POST-WAR YEARS

The 350-year-old link between Croome Court and the Coventrys was finally broken with the sale of the house and its immediate surroundings, including the Pleasure Grounds, in 1948. The family moved into a smaller house at Earls Croome, while Croome Court became a Catholic school and from 1979 a centre for the International Society of Krishna Consciousness. In the drive to make Britain self-sufficient in food, much of Brown's parkland and several of the shrubberies were ploughed up to grow arable crops. The church and the garden buildings inevitably suffered neglect.

Below During the Second World War the eastern part of Croome Park was taken over by RAF Defford

THE EAST LAWN

The restoration of Croome Park is the most ambitious such project ever undertaken by the National Trust. It has been greatly supported in this work by the Heritage Lottery Fund, which has provided both cash and expertise. Volunteers have offered their time and energy in amazingly generous quantities – 25,000 hours since 2002 alone. They have been spurred on by the Friends of Croome, which was set up in 2005 to bring together all those with a passion for Croome. Its president is the garden designer and historian Sir Roy Strong.

Facts and figures

- **45,000** trees and shrubs have been planted, using native and exotic species recorded in the old estate bills and in William Dean's *Hortus Croomensis*.

Above In 2008 the National Trust took on Croome Court – the largest, and most complex, piece in the jigsaw

- **2 miles** of historic paths and carriage drives have been laid to re-establish the traditional route round the Pleasure Grounds and to link the key features.

- **50,000 cubic metres** of silt have been dredged from the river and lake.

- **5 hectares** of new wetland have been created to offset that lost in restoring the historic landscape.

- **160 hectares** of intensively farmed arable land have been returned to wild-flower meadow and pastureland, as conceived by 'Capability' Brown. This process has been supported by the Countryside Stewardship Scheme.

- **17** garden buildings, statues and ornaments have been restored.

- **Rotting wood** from fallen trees has been left as a habitat for beetles, of which Croome has a nationally important population.

- **New visitor facilities** have been made by sympathetically adapting derelict Second World War buildings.

THE FUTURE

A huge amount has been achieved already, but a great deal more remains to be done with your help:

- The ruined ice-house is being rebuilt and re-thatched.
- The Rotunda has to be restored.
- Planting will continue in the woodlands, shelter-belts and orchard.
- The ha-ha is to be restored.
- William Halfpenny's Chinese bridge is to be rebuilt spanning the river.
- Further paths are to be laid across the wider landscape.
- Most importantly of all, the state rooms in the house are to be opened to visitors and gradually redecorated and refurnished.

Below The National Trust has restored the ruined ice-house

Above The National Trust has replanted the Church Shrubbery to revive its late 18th-century appearance

THE COVENTRYS OF CROOME

Sir Thomas Coventry (1547–1606) *buys Croome d'Abitot 1592* = Margaret Jeffery

Thomas , 1st Baron† (1578–1640) Lord Keeper = (1) Sarah Sebright m. 1606
(2) Elizabeth Pitchford m. 1610

Walter = Susanna West

Thomas, 2nd Baron† (1606–61) = Mary Craven† (d. 1634) m. 1627

George, 3rd Baron (1628–80) = Margaret Tufton (1636–) m. 1653

Thomas, 5th Baron (1629–99) = (1) Winifred Edgcumbe (d. 1694)
cr. 1st Earl 1697   (2) Elizabeth Grimes (d. 1724) m. 1695

John, 4th Baron† (1654–85)

Thomas, 2nd Earl (1663–1710) = Anne Somerset (1673–1763) m. 1691

Gilbert, 4th Earl = (1) Dorothy Keyte (d. 1707) m. 1694
(1668–1719)   (2) Anne Masters (1691–1788) m. 1715

Thomas, 3rd Earl (1702–12)

William, 5th Earl (1678–1751) = Elizabeth Allen (d. 1738) m. 1719

Thomas Henry, Viscount Deerhurst (1720–44)

George William, 6th Earl† (1722–1809) = (1) Maria Gunning (1732–60) m. 1752
(2) Barbara St John (1737–1804) m. 1764

George William , 7th Earl† (1758–1831) = (1) Catherine Henley (*c.* 1760–79) m. 1777
(2) Peggy Pitches (d. 1840)

George William , 8th Earl† (1784–1843) = (1) Emma Lygon (d. 1810) m. 1808
(2) Mary Beauclerk (1791–1845) m. 1811

George William, Viscount Deerhurst (1808–38) = Harriet Cockerell (d. 1842) m. 1836

George William, 9th Earl† (1838–1930) = Blanche Gaven (1842–1930) m. 1865

George William, Viscount Deerhurst (1865–1927) = Virginia Bonynge (b. 1866) m. 1894

George William, 10th Earl (1900–40) = Nesta Philipps m. 1921

Charles = Lily Whitehouse

Owners of Croome in Capitals
† indicates monument in Croome Church

George William, 11th Earl (1934–2002)

Francis, 12th Earl (1912–2004)

Bibliography

The Croome Estate Papers are in the Worcestershire Record Office (MS 3671), together with the Burneys' 1784 watercolours. The majority of Adam's drawings for Croome are in Sir John Soane's Museum.

Anon., 'Croome Court', *Country Life*, xiii, 25 April 1903, pp.536–42.

Beard, Geoffrey, 'Robert Adam at Croome Court', *Transactions of the Worcestershire Archaeological Society*, xxxvi, 1958–60, pp.1–5.

Bolton, A.T., 'Croome Court', *Country Life*, xxxvii, 10 April 1915, pp.482–9.

Beresford, Camilla, 'Croome Court, Historic Landscape Survey', unpublished report, 1996.

Colvin, Howard, 'Croome Church and its Architect', *Georgian Group Journal*, viii, 1998, pp.28–32.

David, Penny, *More Hidden Gardens*, Octopus, London, 2004, pp.36–63.

Dean, William et al., *An Historical and Descriptive Account of Croome D'Abitot*, Worcester, 1824.

Gordon, Catherine, *The Coventrys of Croome*, Phillimore, Chichester, 2000.

Grice, Frederick, 'The Park Ornaments of Croome d'Abitot', *Transactions of the Worcestershire Archaeological Society*, 1976, pp.41–9.

Hawkes, William, ed., 'The Diaries of Sanderson Miller of Radway', *Dugdale Society*, xli, 2005.

Kelly, Alison, *Mrs Coade's Stone*, Upton-on-Severn, 1990 (reviewed by Nicholas Penny, *Burlington Magazine*, December 1990, pp.879–80).

Kelly, Alison, 'Coade stone at Croome', *Apollo*, April 1997, pp.21–23.

Meir, Jennifer, *Sanderson Miller and his Landscapes*, Phillimore, Chichester, 2006.

Pike, Andrew, *The Church of St Mary Magdalene, Croome d'Abitot*, Churches Conservation Trust, 2005.

Woodside, Rob, '"Ruinous by Nature": The Archaeology of the Grotto at Croome', *Follies Journal*, no.4, winter 2004, pp.21–5.

Illustrations

Illustrations: Bridgeman Art Library/Musée d'Art et d'Histoire, Geneva p.22 (right); Country Life Picture Library pp.3 (bottom), 28 (bottom); Croome Estate Trust p.28 (top); Croome Estate Trust/Robert Anderson pp.20, 21 (top left), 23 (left); Croome Estate Trust/Edward St Maur Photography pp.2, 3 (top), 22 (left); William Dean, *An Historical and Descriptive Account of Croome D'Abitot*, 1824, pp.7 (bottom), 9 (top), 19 (bottom); Guildhall Library, London p.11 (left); National Portrait Gallery pp.24 (top), 26 (top), 27 (right); National Trust p.29; National Trust Images/Andrew Butler pp.1, 4 (left and right), 5 (right), 9 (bottom), 10 (left and right), 11 (right), 13 (left and right), 14, 15, 16, 17 (right), 21 (bottom left and right), 25 (top), 30, 31 (top and bottom), back cover; NT Images/John Hammond p.24 (bottom); NT Images/David Noton front cover, p.12 (left and right); NT Images/Layton Thompson p.26 (bottom right); NT Images/Rupert Truman p.25 (bottom); Worcestershire Record Office pp.5 (left), 6, 7 (top), 8, 17 (left), 18, 19 (top), 21 (top right), 23 (right), 26 (left), 27 (left).

Acknowledgements

This interim guide is indebted to Catherine Gordon's history of the Coventry family and Camilla Beresford's survey of the historic landscape. I am particularly grateful to Jill Tovey, archivist to the Croome Estate Trust, for her advice and guidance on the immensely rich Croome Estate papers. I would also like to thank the following for their help: Constance Barrett, Geremy Butler, Wendy Carter, Julian Gibbs, Michael Smith, Robin Whittaker and the staffs of the Worcestershire Record Office and the Guildhall Library, London.

Oliver Garnett

© 2008 The National Trust
Reprinted 2011, 2013
Registered charity no. 205846
ISBN 978-1-84359-333-1
Text by Oliver Garnett
Designed by Matt Bourne
Plan of the garden by Imagemaker
Printed by Park Lane Press for National Trust (Enterprises) Ltd,
Heelis, Kemble Drive, Swindon, Wilts SN2 2NA on Cocoon Silk made from 100% recycled paper

The National Trust

is a registered charity

is independent of government

was founded in 1895 to preserve places of historic interest or natural beauty permanently for the benefit of the nation

relies on the generosity of its supporters, through membership subscriptions, gifts, legacies and the contribution of many thousands of volunteers

protects and opens to the public over 300 historic houses and gardens and 49 industrial monuments and mills

owns more than 255,000 hectares (630,000 acres) of the most beautiful countryside and over 710 miles of outstanding coast for people to enjoy

If you would like to become a member or make a donation, please telephone 0844 800 1895 (minicom 0844 800 4410); write to The National Trust, PO Box 574, Rotherham S63 3FH; or see our website at www.nationaltrust.org.uk

Make the most of your visit with this guidebook

Discover how the 6th Earl of Coventry transformed a boggy wasteland into one of the great 18th-century landscape gardens

Enjoy the achievements of his talented team of designers – 'Capability' Brown, Robert Adam and James Wyatt

Learn how the National Trust is bringing Croome back to life

0045556
CSG Croome Park

£4.00

ISBN 978-1-84359-333-1

9 781843 593331